Fairies

Charlotte Guillain

Raintree
Chicago, Illinois

www.heinemannraintree.com
Visit our website to find out more information about Heinemann-Raintree books.

To order:

☎ Phone 888-454-2279

💻 Visit www.heinemannraintree.com to browse our catalog and order online.

© 2011 Raintree
an imprint of Capstone Global Library, LLC
Chicago, Illinois

Edited by Adrian Vigliano, Rebecca Rissman, and Nancy Dickmann
Designed by Joanna Hinton Malivoire
Levelling by Jeanne Clidas
Original illustrations by Christian Slade
Picture research by Elizabeth Alexander
Production by Victoria Fitzgerald
Printed and bound in China by CTPS

14 13 12 11 10
10 9 8 7 6 5 4 3 2 1

Library of Congress Cataloging-in-Publication Data
Guillain, Charlotte.
    Fairies / Charlotte Guillain.
        p. cm.—(Mythical creatures)
    Includes bibliographical references and index.
    ISBN 978-1-4109-3802-2 (hc)—ISBN 978-1-4109-3809-1 (pb) 1. Fairies—Juvenile literature. I. Title.
    BF1552.G86 2011
    398'.45—dc22
                                        2009052415

Acknowledgments
The author and publishers are grateful to the following for permission to reproduce copyright material: Alamy pp. **6** (© Daniel Tückmantel), **14** (© North Wind Picture Archives), **25** (© Photos 12); Corbis pp. **13** (© Christie's Images/ Amelia Jane Murray), **19** (© Bob Sacha), **24** (© Bettmann); Getty Images pp. **11** (SSPL), **20** (Tim Laman/National Geographic); OnAsia Images p. **23** (Jim Goodman); Photolibrary pp. **10** (Andre Skonieczny/imagebroker.net), **18** (Tolo Balaguer/ age footstock), **28** (Andre Skonieczny/imagebroker. net); Rex Features p. **9** (© Dreamworks/Everett); The Bridgeman Art Library pp. **8** (Rackham, Arthur (1867-1939)/ Private Collection/ © Chris Beetles, London, U.K.), **15** (Private Collection); The Kobal Collection p. **29** (ICON PRODUCTIONS).

Some words are shown in bold, **like this**. You can find out what they mean by looking in the glossary.

Contents

What Is a Mythical Creature? 4

What Is a Fairy? 6

The Fairy Myth 10

Fairies of Europe 12

American Little People 16

African Little People 20

Asian Little People 22

Close Relatives 24

Could Fairies Exist? 26

Reality Versus Myth 28

Glossary 30

Find Out More 31

Index 32

What Is a Mythical Creature?

People around the world have told stories for thousands of years. Many of these **myths** are about magical creatures. Could these creatures be real?

DID YOU KNOW?

In ancient China people believed that dragons were friendly creatures that brought good luck.

Have you heard stories about unicorns?
Do you think they could be real?

What Is a Fairy?

The fairies in **myths** are tiny magical creatures that usually look like humans. Many pictures of fairies show them with wings. Today many fairies in books and films are sweet, pretty creatures.

DID YOU KNOW?

Older stories of fairies tell us about little people who made trouble for humans.

7

fairies

Myths tell us fairies have magical powers. People thought fairies stole human babies and replaced them with fairy children. Myths also tell us that fairies play tricks on sleeping humans. Some of these tricks are tangling people's hair or stealing their belongings.

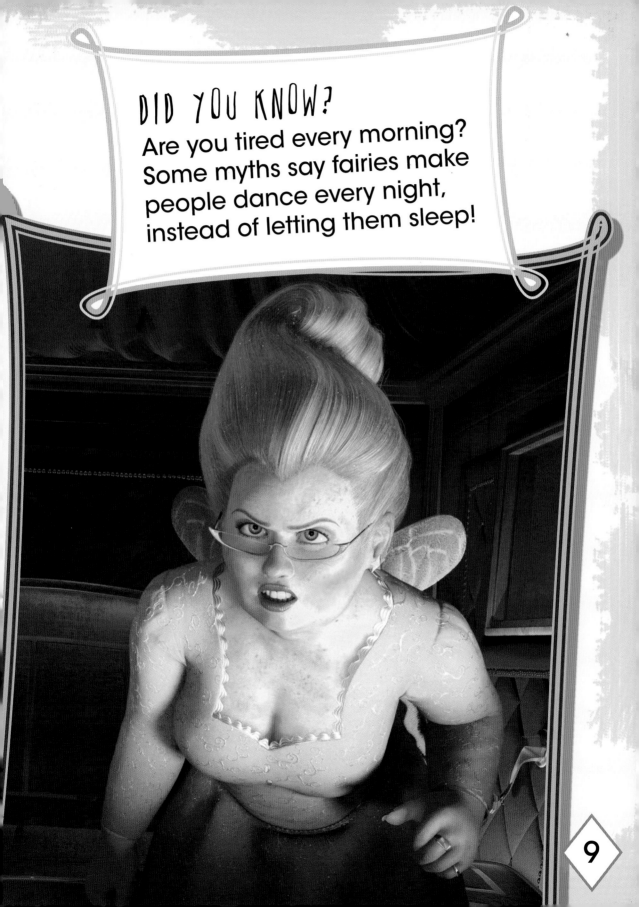

DID YOU KNOW?

Are you tired every morning? Some myths say fairies make people dance every night, instead of letting them sleep!

The Fairy Myth

Some people long ago thought fairies were ghosts. Others thought they were angels. Some people thought fairies had lived on Earth before humans and like to stay hidden. In some countries, there are stories of magical "little people" who are similar to fairies.

lacewing

DID YOU KNOW?

People may have seen insects, such as lacewings, and thought they were flying fairies.

This photograph was taken by two girls in 1917. Many people were tricked into believing that the fairy in the photograph was real.

11

Fairies of Europe

Myths in Ireland and Scotland say fairies are tiny **immortal** creatures who hide from humans. These fairies live underground or inside hills. The myths tell people to stay away from places where fairies live so they don't disturb the little creatures.

Scotland

Ireland

Europe

DID YOU KNOW?

People thought they could keep fairies away:
- with cold iron
- by wearing clothes inside out
- by ringing bells

clurichauns

Scottish **myths** say that fairies pinch people who live in dirty houses. Irish myths tell of fairies called clurichauns (say *clue-reh-kahns*). The pooka (say *pooh-kah*) is another Irish fairy. It could change into a horse and take farmers' crops.

Stories say leprechauns (say *lep-reh-kahns*) are Irish fairies who guard treasure. Some people wanted to catch leprechauns to get their gold.

leprechaun

American Little People

Many Native American **myths** tell of fairylike "little people." The Lakota people have myths about little creatures living in trees, called canotila (say *can-oh-tee-la*). Iroquois Indian myths tell about nature **spirits**, called jogah (say *joh-gah*). They help keep nature balanced.

North America

Canada

Central America

Mexico

canotila

DID YOU KNOW?
In Newfoundland, Canada, people thought they could keep fairies away with a slice of bread!

In Mexico there are Aztec **myths** about the chaneque (say *chah-neh-keh*). These little people look after nature. The only way to their underground world is through a kapok tree. Mayan stories from Central America tell of tiny creatures called aluxob (say *all-ush-ob*). They can become invisible!

chaneque

kapok tree

DID YOU KNOW?

Mayan farmers build little houses for aluxob so the fairies will help their crops grow.

19

African Little People

In southern Africa, Zulu people have **myths** about little people called the abatwa (say *ah-bat-wah*). They live in anthills and ride around on ants. In West Africa, stories tell of tiny forest **spirits** called aziza (say *ah-zee-zah*). They use their magic to help hunters.

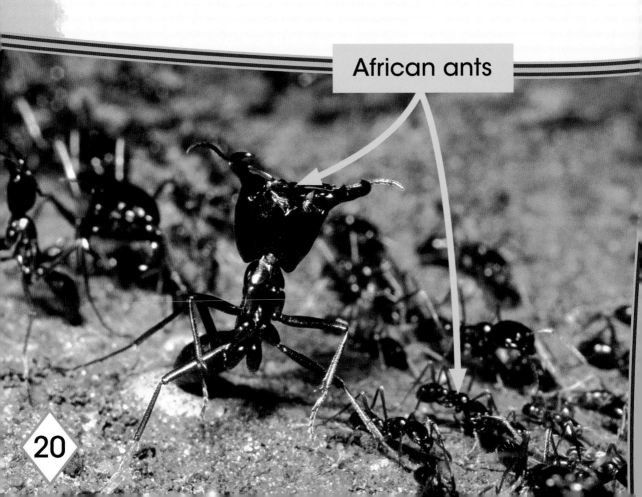

African ants

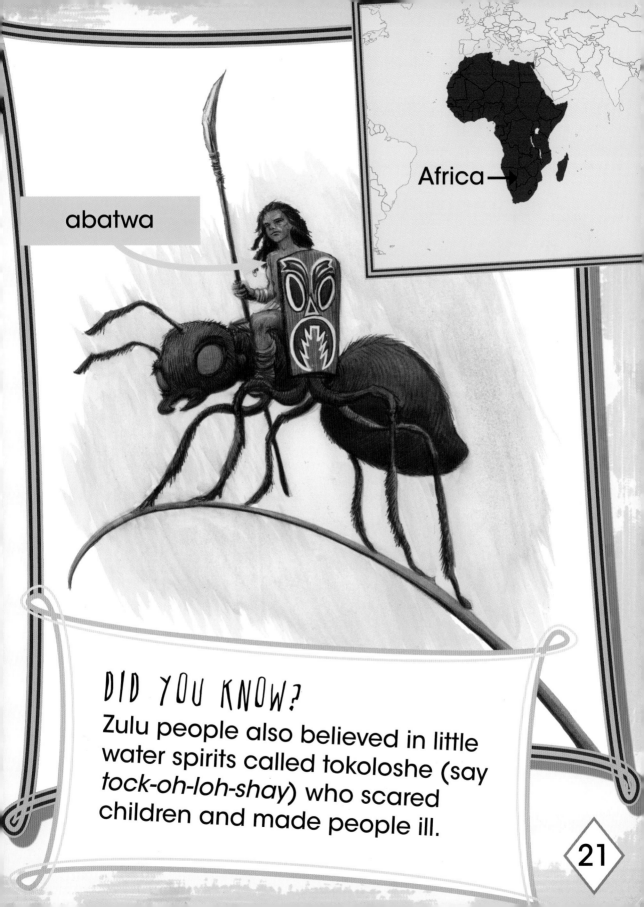

abatwa

Africa→

DID YOU KNOW?

Zulu people also believed in little water spirits called tokoloshe (say *tock-oh-loh-shay*) who scared children and made people ill.

Asian Little People

People in many Asian countries tell stories about little people. In the Philippines, there is a **myth** about diwata (say *dee-wah-tah*). They live in trees and help people who look after forests and mountains. But they **punish** humans who harm nature!

diwata

These Nu people are at a Fairy Festival.

Asia →

China →

Philippines →

DID YOU KNOW?

In China the Nu people have a Fairy Festival for three days every March. They give gifts to fairies to help the crops grow.

23

Close Relatives

Many other **mythical** creatures around the world are similar to fairies. Stories say brownies are small creatures that live in Scottish houses. People believed brownies did jobs around the house at night if they gave them food.

Goblins are like fairies, too.

goblins

DID YOU KNOW?

Some stories describe beautiful elves who live in forests and caves. They have magical powers and look after nature.

Could Fairies Exist?

What do you think?

 They could be real...

- Some people say they have seen fairies and even taken photos of them.

 I'm not so sure...

- You can't believe everything people say. Many photos of fairies turn out to be **hoaxes.**

 They could be real...

- Fairies use magic to hide from us.

 I'm not so sure...

- Nobody has seen fairies using magic, so we can't prove this.

They could be real...

- People all over the world have stories about little people, so they must be real.

 I'm not so sure...

- Lots of stories around the world are similar. It doesn't mean the stories are true.

The truth is that fairies don't really exist. But they make a great story!

27

Reality Versus Myth

Lacewing (real)

Found: North America and Europe

Lives: In gardens, parks, meadows, and forests

Features: Green body, golden eyes, delicate wings

Special power: Can make a disgusting smell

Seen: At night between May and August

Fairy (myth)

Found: All over the world

Lives: In forests and underground caves

Features: Very small, looks like a human, may have wings

Special power: Magic

Seen: In movies and in books

Glossary

hoax trick

immortal someone or something that will never die

metal hard shiny material

myth traditional story, often about magical creatures and events

mythical found in myths

punish make someone suffer because they have done something wrong

spirit magical creature

Find Out More

Books

Colfer, Eoin. *Artemis Fowl*. London, UK: Puffin, 2006.

Maloney, Alison. *Fairies*. New York, NY: Sterling Publishing: 2008.

Reinhart, Matthew and Sabuda, Robert. *Encyclopedia Mythologica*. Cambridge, MA: Candlewick Press, 2008.

Websites

www.artemisfowl.co.uk
Find out more about the fairies in the world of Artemis Fowl at this Website.

www.rainbowmagiconline.com
Visit this Website to find out more about the Rainbow Magic series of books about fairies. There are activities and games to play and you can even create your own fairy!

Index

abatwa 20
Africa 20, 21
aluxob 18, 19
Asia 22, 23
aziza 20

brownies 24

canotila 16
Central America 18
chaneque 18
clurichauns 14
crops 14, 19, 23

diwata 22

elves 25
Europe 12, 13, 14, 15, 28

Fairy Festival 23
forests 20, 22, 25, 28, 29

hoaxes 27

jogah 16

lacewings 10, 28
leprechauns 15

magical powers 8, 20, 25, 26, 27, 29
myths 4, 6, 8, 9, 10, 12, 14, 16, 18, 20, 22, 24, 29

North America 28

pookas 14

sizes 6, 12, 18, 20, 24, 29

tokoloshe 21
treasure 15

wings 6, 28, 29